The Collector's Guide to
# American Indian Artifacts

# The Collector's Guide to
# American Indian Artifacts

LLOYD C. HARNISHFEGER

illustrated by
SANDRA HEINEN

Lerner Publications Company
Minneapolis

*For Marjorie and Rebecca*

LIBRARY OF CONGRESS CATALOGING IN PUBLICATION DATA

Harnishfeger, Lloyd.
The collector's guide to American Indian artifacts.

SUMMARY: An introduction to collecting Indian relics, covering such topics as where to hunt for them, how to identify them, how to clean, mount, display, and catalog them, and how to restore broken artifacts.

Includes index.     Bibliography: pp. 93-94

1. Indians of North America—Antiquities—Collectors and collecting—United States—Juvenile literature. 2. Indians of North America—Implements—Juvenile literature. 3. United States—Antiquities—Juvenile literature. [1. Indians of North America—Antiquities—Collectors and collecting] I. Title.

E77.92.H37 1975          973'.04'97          74-33525
ISBN 0-8225-0759-5

Published simultaneously in Canada by J. M. Dent & Sons (Canada) Ltd., Don Mills, Ontario.

Manufactured in the United States of America

International Standard Book Number: 0-8225-0759-5
Library of Congress Catalog Card Number: 74-33525

# Contents

# Preface

Stone artifacts made by the North American Indians and their prehistoric ancestors can be found all over the continental United States. Museums and private collections contain thousands of weapons, tools, and ornaments made by these amazingly skillful craftsmen. And in some sections of the country, there is hardly a family that does not have a small personal collection of Indian relics.

Despite the fact that so many of these relics exist, very little has been written about them. Some highly technical volumes have been published, but there are few books on this subject that are written in everyday language for beginning collectors. It is hoped that this volume will help to fill the need for an introductory book about collecting Indian relics.

The material in the pages that follow is not meant to be all-inclusive. In fact, this book can but scratch the surface of the subject. But it will provide the reader with some general knowledge about the artifacts most commonly found in the United States. Suggestions about how to find, display, and restore these artifacts are included as well.

Readers will notice that in this book, frequent use is made of phrases such as "it is believed . . ." or "most scholars think. . . ." This has been necessary since much of the material included is based on opinion; factual information about the Indians and prehistoric peoples of

North America is still quite scarce. We do know, however, that the history of these people stretches far back into the distant past. Most experts accept the theory that ancestors of the Indians came to North America from Asia, walking across a land "bridge" (now the Bering Strait) that connected the two continents. But there is considerable disagreement among authorities as to how long ago this migration occurred. Fossil evidence has led many scholars to conclude that humans first crossed the Bering Strait more than 15,000 years ago. Other evidence, less widely accepted, pushes the date back to over 25,000 years ago. At any rate, it is safe to say that the Indians' ancestors were living in North America many thousands of years before the arrival of the first Europeans.

Unfortunately, most of the early Americans' long history has gone unrecorded. Even at the time of European arrival in America, the native Americans had no written language. And in many cases their wandering way of life did little to encourage any kind of permanent architecture. For these reasons and others, we must depend largely on the tools and weapons that they left behind to tell us something about their way of life.

Many logical theories have been put forward that suggest how the Indians and their ancestors may have lived and what purposes were served by the items they made. These theories are based on the discoveries that are constantly being made by archaeologists, anthropologists, and many serious amateur collectors. As time goes on, new discoveries will continue to provide us with new information, and we will gradually replace our educated guesses with facts.

Finally, it should be noted that as new discoveries are made, some of the opinions expressed in this book will undoubtedly be proven wrong. But discovering a mistake is not so tragic if correcting that mistake leads to knowledge of the truth.

# Part one
# Becoming a Collector

The following chapters provide a basic introduction to the hobby of collecting North American Indian artifacts. Beginning collectors will learn where and how to hunt for relics, how to keep accurate records of their finds, and how to identify the artifacts in their collections. Also included are instructions for displaying and restoring stone artifacts.

As the beginning collector gains experience, he or she will undoubtedly develop new methods for approaching the many aspects of collecting. But it is hoped that the guidelines presented here will provide collectors with a solid groundwork that will prove useful to them both as beginners and in the future.

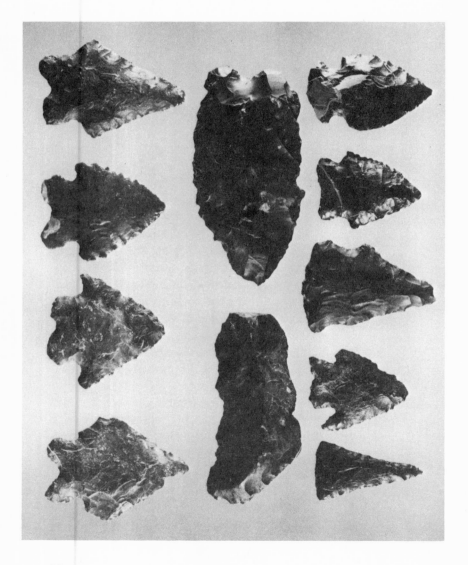

# 1.
# Collecting Artifacts as a Hobby

Collecting Indian relics is a rewarding pastime for people of all ages and interests. This hobby requires no special skills or training—only perseverance and a desire to learn. In fact, if your eyesight is reasonably good and if you are willing to do some walking, then you fulfill all the requirements for becoming a hunter and finder of ancient Indian relics.

When you become a relic hunter, you may choose to hunt either in a group or alone. Perhaps you like to "get away from it all." If so, field hunting by yourself can be a relaxing time of solitude that is very rewarding, regardless of the amount of success you may have on the hunt. On the other hand, if you enjoy being with people on an outing, you are sure to find others who are already hunters, or who would like to begin hunting. Amateur archaeological clubs may already be organized somewhere near your area. If not, placing a classified advertisement in your newspaper will undoubtedly attract enough people to start a collectors' group.

Relic hunting appeals to many people because it is a hobby without expenses. Unlike fishing, bowling, or team sports, relic hunting requires no special equipment or supplies. There are no dues to pay, no licenses to buy, and no admission fees. Since you will be hunting only for relics that can be found on the ground's surface, you will not need digging tools. The only equipment you will need is a pair of good walking shoes (or boots), an old toothbrush, a magnifying glass, a plastic bag, and perhaps some mosquito repellent.

In addition to being an inexpensive outdoor activity, relic hunting is also an educational hobby. Hunting for relics will invariably lead you to an interest in the history of the artifacts that you find. You will ask yourself questions about the people who made and used these items. Where did the people come from, and where did they go? How did they obtain food and clothing? What kinds of games did they play? What were their homes like?

You can find the answers to these and many other questions by reading books about the lives of the American Indians and their prehistoric ancestors. As you search through these sources, you will see connections between historical accounts and the relics you have found. You will begin to feel a true kinship with people who lived in your area hundreds, perhaps even thousands, of years ago.

Relic hunting may also cause you to wonder why certain types of stone were chosen for the manufacture of tools and weapons. Questions like this might lead you to study geology and the properties of various rocks and minerals. Such background research has an added advantage: it is an activity that you can pursue all year round, even when cold winter weather makes outdoor hunting impossible.

Indian relic collecting is a rewarding hobby for all of the reasons given above. But its greatest appeal is in the excitement it can provide. There is nothing quite like the feeling you will have when you discover that first perfect arrowhead, spear point, axe, or knife. You will agree that it is a never-to-be-forgotten moment—one that you will want to experience again and again as the years go by.

# 2.
# How to Begin

"Experience is the best teacher" is an old saying and a true one. Therefore, one of the best ways to get started as a collector is by talking with experienced relic hunters and collectors in your area. Long-time residents of your community will probably be able to provide you with the names and addresses of these collectors. Once you learn who and where the collectors are, a telephone call will often be all that is necessary to obtain an invitation to see their collections. Most collectors are happy to show their artifacts to anyone who is sincerely interested in them.

When you call a collector, you might simply say that you have learned of his or her interest in Indian relics and that, as a beginner, you would like to ask for help and advice in getting started. More often than not, the collector will invite you to see his or her collection of artifacts. Take advantage of this opportunity if it is offered, for during the visit you can learn a lot from the collector about where and how to hunt.

The greatest benefit of such a visit is the chance to see, firsthand, the types, shapes, and colors of the various artifacts found in the area you will be covering. Beginning field hunters often fail to recognize relics that are partly buried in the ground, slightly broken, or oddly shaped. If you can examine many types of artifacts in an experienced hunter's collection, you will have a better idea of what to look for. Then you will be less likely to miss or to discard valuable relics in the field.

In addition to showing you his or her artifacts, the collector may invite you to come along on a hunt at some future time. This is the very best way to learn, so accept the invitation if you can.

Talking with experienced collectors is the best way to get off to a good start as a relic hunter. But there are also many other ways in which you can help yourself to become successful in the field.

A visit to your local museum can provide information about where the best hunting areas may be. Pay particular attention to any Indian relic exhibits that include information about the donor of the items or about where the artifacts were found. It is a good idea to jot down these names and locations. You may be able to use them later when you are planning where to hunt. It is generally true that where some relics have been found, others still exist.

If there is a state or local relic collectors' group in your area, you will probably find it helpful to attend any exhibits they may be planning.

Studying various maps can be useful, too. You can start by looking at an ordinary road map of your state. Note the positions and courses of the major rivers and their tributaries in the area where you hope to search. It is a good idea to watch for villages and towns that have Indian names, since these names were undoubtedly chosen in honor of the earlier inhabitants of the region. Parks, forts, and historical landmarks will be shown on the map, and you should take note of those that relate to the history of the Indians who once lived in your area. County and township maps may also be helpful if they are available.

Your public library and its staff will be able to provide you with more leads. If you tell the librarians in the reference department what kind of information you need, they will make available any material that they feel may be useful.

Finally, arrange to travel through your own immediate vicinity. Take note of the condition of the cultivated fields, of crops that have been planted, and of the general "lay of the land." Look for obvious knolls, river bottoms, and plateau areas. As you move through the country looking for the most likely places to begin hunting, keep the following points in mind.

1.  The Indians had to have sources of water near their camps and villages. The containers they used (generally made of fired clay, bark, or animal skins) were not suitable for carrying or storing large amounts of water. For this reason you'll probably have your best luck within a mile of a lake, river, spring, or marsh, or in areas where such water sources once existed.

2.  Most Indian tribes of more recent times (approximately the last 1,200 years) did some simple farming for at least a part of each year. Therefore, areas of fertile, easily worked soil were chosen for village and camp sites. Good soil was necessary, since the people who worked the ground used only simple hoes and grubbing tools of wood, stone, or bone.

3.  Indian camps were usually located on hills and ridges. This was true for several reasons, the most obvious of which was the need for drainage and protection from floods. On level or low ground, a good, hard rain could turn a floorless house of bark or skins into a very muddy and miserable place to be! In addition to the need for drainage, safety was probably another reason for locating settlements

on hills. The higher ground was easier to defend in case of attack. Because the hill allowed a good view of the surrounding countryside, an enemy would have had trouble trying to surprise the village.

For these reasons it is usually wise to begin hunting on high, fertile ground that is near a source of water. This is not to say, however, that relics cannot be found on lower or level ground. The Indians traveled great distances in all directions from their camps in order to pursue game, to search for food, and to make war. Wherever they went, they lost weapons and tools.

No matter where you choose to hunt, you should be aware of the laws governing ownership of relics found in the area. For example, some states claim ownership of all relics found in that state. Other states claim rights to artifacts found on public lands only. Most states have no such "antiquities laws," but any beginner should be sure to find out what is legal in his or her state. A letter to your state's archaeological society should provide a quick answer to this important question.

When you have picked out a few promising hunting areas and when you feel that you have done enough background research, you are ready to choose a site for your first hunt.

# 3.
# Your First Hunt

Do your best to make sure that your first hunt is successful. If it isn't, you may become discouraged and feel that there are no relics to be found or that you are unable to spot them. Therefore, pick the most promising area for your first trip. The ground should be well worked down, and fairly smooth and level. Ideally, at least one good, hard rain should have fallen on the field within two weeks before the time you hunt it. The falling rain levels and smooths the soil, and cleans off any stones that are lying on the surface. This cleaning reveals the true shape and form of the stones, and makes them much easier to identify.

When you have located a cultivated field that looks promising, you should, of course, stop and ask the owner if you may hunt for Indian relics on his or her farm. Some landowners believe that collectors will be *digging* for artifacts, and they are understandably reluctant to give their permission. For this reason, it is important to let the owner know that you will be hunting only for items that can be seen on the ground's surface.

Before you begin, you should be sure that you know the boundaries of the owner's land. It is also important to take note of any special instructions the owner may give you as to which fields you should not enter, which gates should be closed or left open, etc. Of course you must honor all these requests, or you will certainly not be welcome to hunt there a second time.

Now you are ready to begin hunting. Pick the part of the field that looks the most promising, and hunt it carefully and thoroughly. As you walk, do not try to cover a path more than six feet wide. Walk very slowly, and keep your vision swinging back and forth across the narrow path you are hunting. When you reach the end of the field, move over about six feet and walk back. Continue this process until you have searched the entire area.

Many artifacts that collectors find in the field are broken, like the arrowhead fragments shown above.

Examine every stone that looks in any way as if it might have been used by people. Pick the stone up and remove any clinging soil, which may hide grooves, notches, chipped edges, grinding marks, or other evidence of work or wear on the piece.

Flint and closely related types of stone, such as chert, chalcedony, and jasper, are probably the easiest to recognize in the field. These stones have smooth, shiny surfaces and distinctive colors. They may be black, white, gray, blue, brown, tan, yellow, pink, red, orange, or a combination of these colors. It is very fortunate for the hunter that these stones are so colorful and easy to spot, because the Indians made great numbers of weapon points and tools from such stones. The relics can be found in all shapes, and they vary in size from tiny "bird points" less than ½ inch long to huge knives and spearheads up to 10 inches long.

On your first hunt, keep all the flint pieces, chips, and flakes that you find, even if they do not appear to be worked at all. (A small plastic bag makes a good carry-all for smaller items of this kind.) Don't spend too much time examining your finds in the field. Wait until you get home, where you can wash them. You can study each piece carefully then.

# 4.

# Cleaning and Recording Your Artifacts

When you get home, scrub each of your relics carefully under running water. An old toothbrush is ideal for this purpose. It will do a good job of removing soil from the cracks and notches in the stone.

When each stone is dry, examine all its sides and edges carefully with a magnifying glass. There is a good chance that some of the flint pieces that at first looked like useless scrap will show minute chipping and flaking along one edge. Such chipping proves that an item is a worked piece (perhaps a scraper or knife) and that it should become part of your collection.

Undoubtedly, most of the flint chips and flakes you've saved will be of no value. But the fact that you saw these clearly enough to collect them will prove your ability to recognize the kind of stone most commonly used to make tools and weapons. This should be encouraging to you, and it is good practice for your future hunting trips.

Recording your finds is the next step, and it should be done just as soon as possible after the hunt. It is amazing how quickly you can forget where and when various items were found if you do not make the necessary records immediately. The historical and monetary value of your collection will be largely determined by the amount of care you take with your record-keeping. In fact, the greatest single problem with many so-called collections is the absence of accurate records telling where and when each relic was found.

A looseleaf notebook filled with unlined paper makes the best log book for listing and describing your finds. The information in your notebook need not be elaborate. It will usually take only a few minutes to log in the findings of a day's hunt.

After each field hunting trip, list the exact location at which you hunted, and the date. Then, trace around each of your new artifacts with a pencil, and write down anything unusual about each item. Assign a code letter to each location, and a number to each item that you have found. For example, if you call the Jones farm "site A," and you have found three arrowheads there, then you will label those arrowheads "A-1," "A-2," and "A-3." These code numbers should be printed within the traced outline on the notebook page.

The numbers should also be printed on the artifacts themselves. You can simply print the code numbers on small squares of adhesive tape, which can then be stuck onto each artifact.

After you have recorded your data, you will want to put it in some kind of orderly arrangement. A looseleaf notebook is best for listing your finds because it allows you to arrange your information in a logical way simply by changing the order of the pages. For example, suppose that you want to arrange your notebook to show the variety of relics found at one particular site. Perhaps you have hunted at site A on May 15, at site B on May 25, at site C on June 5, and then at site A again on June 15. If you have recorded your finds correctly after each trip, there will be several pages separating information about the two hunts made at site A. With a looseleaf notebook, the problem is easily solved by rearranging the pages so that all of your findings from site A are grouped together.

No matter how large your log book may become, it can always be logically organized.

If your book is kept up well from year to year, you will begin to see a true picture of the types of artifacts found at each site. By studying your records, any interested persons will be able to draw accurate conclusions about the tribes and classes of people who once lived in the area. This is the purpose of the information recorded in the log book—to provide permanent records for your own use, as well as for anyone else who may be interested.

Unfortunately, many field hunters do not keep adequate records, and some keep no records at all. Professional archaeologists strongly disapprove of this. And they are especially critical of amateur collectors who dig into ancient mounds and village sites for the sole purpose of carrying away any artifacts that may lie buried there. Such "pot hunters" as these deserve all the abuse the professionals give them. For once any artifact is removed from its resting place, a bit of history has been destroyed forever.

The best advice that can be given an amateur, then, is to *keep good, written records*, and don't *dig* at all unless a trained person is supervising the work.

# 5.
# Identification and Classification

Although the recording of your artifacts should always be completed immediately, there is no hurry as far as classification is concerned. In fact, it is probable that the longer you take to classify your artifacts, the more accurate your classification will be.

Classification is the process of grouping artifacts into categories according to their common characteristics. Most of the artifacts that you will find can be grouped into several major categories, or types. Some common types include scrapers, knives, and projectile points, or weapon tips. In some cases, careful examination of the details of an artifact will lead you to further classify it in a specific sub-category. For example, you may initially identify a relic with one sharpened side as a scraper. Upon closer examination, you will notice that the artifact is notched in a particular way. This will enable you to classify it more precisely as a "hafted" scraper.

Classifying relics is often difficult for the beginning collector, and your first attempts may be incorrect or incomplete. But do the best you can by using the information you've gathered from library research, museum trips, and talks with collectors. Later on, as you gain knowledge and experience, you can go back and correct or add to the information in your records.

Three things must be considered when you attempt to classify a stone tool or weapon. These are its shape, the raw material from which it is made, and the working technique used by its maker.

The most obvious characteristic of any relic is its shape. Stone tools and weapons can be found in a wide variety of forms, and many of them can be identified by their shapes alone. A stone pestle, for example, is a bell-shaped grinding tool with a flared base and a rounded handle. Its shape can be readily distinguished from that of a common stone drill, which is long and narrow with a point at one end. Some artifacts, such as axes, have grooves or notches that give them a distinctive shape. These grooves were worked into stone artifacts so that they could be fastened to a shaft or handle. The shape and placement of these grooves — or the absence of them — can be helpful in identifying many stone items. (Descriptions of the distinctive shapes and sizes of various individual artifacts can be found in Part II of this book.)

After taking note of the shape of a relic, you should then identify the raw material of which the relic is made. Most artifacts that you find will be made of some variety of flint, but you may also find items made of slate, granite, quartz, or other stone. The material from which a tool or weapon is fashioned often provides the basis for classification of the relic.

Your third consideration should be the technique used to make the artifact. Although many of the ancient secrets of working stone are lost forever, we do know the basic methods that were used. Different cultures, different tribes, and probably even different individuals made their artifacts in various ways. But most of them followed the same basic steps. By learning to recognize these basic methods, you can do a more accurate job of identifying your artifacts.

*Percussion-flaking* was the earliest and crudest method

of shaping flint tools. To begin this process, a block of flint, called a *core*, was struck repeatedly with a hammer-stone. The core may have been partly buried in the ground to keep it steady, or perhaps it was held between the feet, as is still done in certain primitive societies today.

The force of the blows was directed toward the edges of the flint core. Eventually a stone flake flew off the side of the core. This flake was then battered roughly into shape by striking it along the edges with a small "hammer"

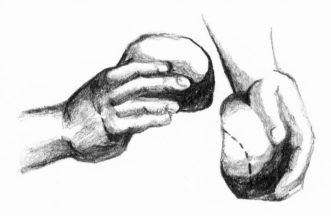

Percussion-flaking. *Top*: Pounding a flake loose from the core stone. *Below*: Using a hammerstone to shape the flake into a crude tool.

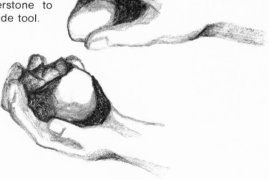

made of stone or bone. The people of some cultures stopped at this point in the work, and so their artifacts usually look heavy and rather crude.

Other groups carried the work one step further, especially in the manufacture of knife blades and projectile points. After percussion-flaking was completed, the piece was refined by *pressure-flaking*. To do this, the maker held the roughly formed artifact in one hand and,

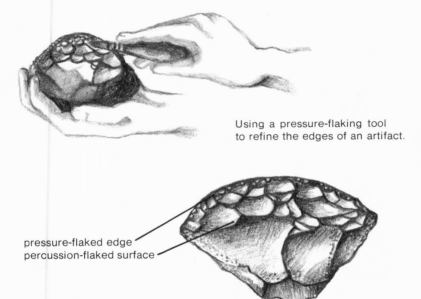

Using a pressure-flaking tool to refine the edges of an artifact.

pressure-flaked edge
percussion-flaked surface

using a small pointed tool of deer horn or bone, carefully chipped the edges into a fine, sharp blade or point.

It is popularly believed that the Indians spent hours and hours chipping away at their flint rocks in order to turn out a finished implement. Actually, it has been demonstrated many times that the entire process can be completed in a matter of minutes! The procedure is simple, but anyone who tries to *master* this art will soon gain a new and deeper respect for those early hunters' work. The implements they made were not only serviceable, but often very beautiful as well.

When you examine your artifacts, determine which chipping techniques were used to make them. If the flaking scars are large and irregularly spaced, you can usually conclude that percussion-flaking was used. Small, regularly spaced scars usually indicate the use of pressure-flaking. Look to see if most of the scars meet near the center of the artifact. If they do, they probably form a *spine*, which is characteristic of certain kinds of projectile points. Finally, use a magnifying glass to check the edges of the piece. The quality of the chipping done on this area will often help you to classify the artifact.

The chipping techniques discussed above were used largely in making items of flint. Artifacts made of stone other than flint were often fashioned by a method called *pecking and polishing*. Unlike the chipping techniques,

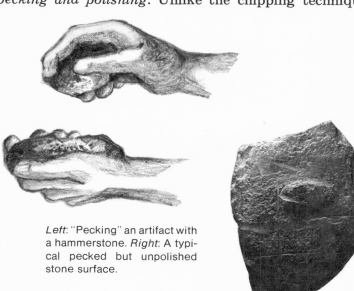

*Left*: "Pecking" an artifact with a hammerstone. *Right*: A typical pecked but unpolished stone surface.

this method was quite time-consuming. The maker began by finding a smooth, hard stone (usually speckled granite) that was nearly the right size for the intended tool. The maker would then begin "pecking" at the surface wherever he or she wished to change the shape. Pecking was done by tapping at the rock with a small hammerstone, which was held in the hand. As the light, tapping blows continued, tiny grains and chips of stone broke off. In time, the stone began to take the desired shape. The pecking method often produced a pockmarked surface, which can clearly be seen on many axe heads and other tools.

When the tool was roughly shaped, the long process of grinding began. The Indian did this by rubbing the tool on another stone or by using a small stone to rub and polish the tool until it was smooth and sharp. The "ground stone" items made by this method will have smooth, even surfaces. The more refined artifacts will sometimes be highly polished as well. This polishing was probably done with a piece of sandstone, or possibly with a handful of loose sand.

The three considerations discussed above—shape, type of raw material, and working technique—will be your basic guidelines for identifying and classifying the stone artifacts in your collection. In addition to these general guidelines, the descriptions of individual artifacts in Part II will be of further help to you in recognizing and naming specific types of tools and projectile points.

# 6.
# Mounting, Display, and Storage

One of the things that you will enjoy most about your relic collection will be the chance to show some of your finds to your friends. This calls for a method of display that will bring out the true beauty of your relics.

*Picture framing* works very well for smaller items, such as arrowheads, drills, scrapers, and knives.

1.  Select a picture frame, and choose a backing board of thin plywood or masonite cut to a size that fits the frame.
2.  Cut a piece of material (felt and velveteen are best) two inches wider and two inches longer than the backing board.
3.  Lay the backing board face down in the center of the material and run a heavy line of white glue around the outer edges of the board's back side.
4.  Fold the overlapping flaps of material over onto the wet glue. (You may want to cut a slit in the extra material at the corners. This will help to make the corners lie flat.) Pull on each flap of material to remove wrinkles.
5.  Weight the board with books or some other heavy objects and allow it to dry overnight.
6.  When the glue is dry, try different arrangements

of your best relics by placing them on the material in various ways. A dark background material such as red, black, dark blue, or dark green will be best for displaying a group of white or light-colored items. Choose a white or neutral background for groups of black or dark-colored relics.

7. When you have decided on a design grouping, place a drop of glue on several of the highest points of the back of each artifact (the side you do not want to show), and press each one firmly into the background material. Allow the glue to dry overnight.

8. Hang the completed display as you would any small, framed picture.

A variation of the picture framing method of display is called *plaque mounting*. This is especially effective for displaying a single artifact, such as a large spearhead. First, select a piece of wood in a color that will contrast nicely with the relic you want to display. The wood can then be cut in a variety of shapes, such as squares, rectangles, circles, triangles, or arrowheads. Next, smooth the wood by sanding it, especially around the cut edges, and then finish it in any way you like. You may want to varnish it, or simply to leave it unfinished. Finally, use white glue to mount your artifact directly on the completed plaque.

Wall plaques will display many of your artifacts very nicely, but they will not be suitable for very heavy items. Bookends displaying two or more of your heavier relics are easy to make and will prove to be very useful. You can simply glue your artifact onto the base of any wooden bookend. The weight of the stone is just what is needed to keep the bookends from slipping apart when holding several books. In addition to their usefulness, they will look interesting and attractive on your desk or bookcase.

Since you will want to display only your best relics,

A granite game ball (2-5/8 inches in diameter) mounted on a wooden bookend

you must find some method for storing the others. You can keep them in any box, drawer, or chest. But some kind of padding and separation must be provided, because many relics are fragile and can break easily.

Small-parts chests, such as those used by mechanics and repairmen, are fine for storing small drills, bird points, thumb scrapers, etc. The clear plastic drawers in these chests usually come supplied with movable dividers, and the drawers themselves can be labeled for quick reference to each item that they contain. A piece of soft cloth placed in the bottom of each drawer will protect even your most delicate artifacts.

No matter where you decide to store your unmounted relics, a definite plan should be followed for grouping them. Two common methods of organization are:

1. Grouping by location (all items found on the same site or area are kept together).
2. Grouping by type (all projectile points together, all drills together, all scrapers together, etc.). When possible, you may want to further divide and group your relics into sub-categories (all hafted scrapers together, all side scrapers together, etc.).

Either of these plans is satisfactory, but grouping by location will probably follow more closely the basic plan of your log book. Organizing by location will also prove to be more informative to anyone who is interested in knowing where each item was found.

# 7.
# Restoring Broken Artifacts

Unfortunately, a large number of Indian relics found today are broken. Many were probably broken while their makers were using them. Some artifacts have been damaged gradually by actions of nature, such as repeated freezing and thawing. And others have been struck by farm implements and machinery during cultivation of the fields in which they lie. No matter how an artifact came to be broken, it should probably be restored in some way to its original size and shape.

Some people might consider this practice unethical or dishonest. But there is absolutely nothing wrong with restoring an artifact, provided that the finished piece is then labeled "restored." Collectors who repair an incomplete specimen are not doing so in order to fool anyone. Their only purpose is to make the relic look as nearly like it once did as possible.

Of course, you should not attempt to restore an artifact unless you are reasonably sure of its original shape. This is no problem if, for example, only the tip of an arrow point is missing, or if one barb has broken off. But when large sections of an artifact are gone, you should seek expert advice before attempting any repair work.

You should also be very sure that the "broken" piece you are going to mend is really broken, and not a special type of tool that was made in that way to begin with. The hafted scraper, for example, is an artifact that was fashioned from a broken arrowhead. Its maker carefully reworked the broken point into a scraping edge (see Part II). But a careless person might mistake a hafted scraper

These five restored artifacts are ready for painting. The light sections are water putty.

for a damaged arrowhead. "Restoring" such a piece by adding a point would only result in the loss of a fine relic.

Restoring broken artifacts is not difficult, but it does require patience and practice. If all the pieces of a broken relic are available, you may simply glue the pieces back together. Almost any good slow-drying glue will be satisfactory. But when a part or section of the relic is missing, a patch will have to be made to take its place.

Plaster of paris will usually make a good patch, but some collectors prefer other materials, such as a furnace cement or powdered, water-soluable putty. The author has found that Durham's Rock Hard Water Putty works very well for almost any kind of repair job. It is available at most hardware stores, paint stores, and hobby shops.

It is best to do your first repair job on a small item. So, let us imagine that you want to repair a small arrowhead from which the point is missing. The following method will restore the artifact to a good likeness of its original shape.

1. Mix the water putty by adding the powder *to the water*. For best results, add three parts powder to one part water. (It is not necessary to use more than a teaspoonful of water for small repairs such as this one.) Add the powder a little at a time, and keep stirring. As you stir, rap the container on the table top occasionally. This will bring any bubbles to the surface. The bubbles should then be broken. If this is not done, the air pockets will make holes in the material after it hardens. The mixture should be smooth and slightly stiff before you stop adding powder. The putty is ready to apply when it is stiff enough to handle without sticking to your fingers.

2. Using a small knife or your fingers, press a blob of the thick paste onto the arrowhead to replace the missing point.

3. Lay the relic on some newspaper and allow it to dry until it is hard to the touch, but still damp.

4. Shape the repaired portion roughly with a sharp knife or a single-edged razor blade.

5. Allow the relic to dry overnight.

6. Finish the piece by carving, grinding, and sanding the patch to the shape desired. Try to match the surface texture of the stone, as well as to form the

correct shape of the arrow point. (If the patch should happen to break loose from the stone while you are working on it, simply glue it back into place.)

7. Paint the patched portion with artist's oil paints mixed to the color of the original artifact.

Once you have learned the basic techniques of restoration by working on small jobs, restoring larger items will not be difficult. This same basic method can be used to patch broken axes, bannerstones, gorgets, or almost any other kind of stone relic.

# 8.
# The Value of
# Your Collection

One of the most common questions that collectors are asked about Indian relics is, "What are they worth?" This is a difficult question to answer, because one person's idea of what is valuable will never be the same as another's. Assuming, however, that the question refers to the value of an artifact if sold today on the open market, we may make some very *general* statements about determining worth.

The value of anything is decided by two factors: supply (how plentiful is it?) and demand (how desirable is it?). Gold, for example, is very valuable because our supply of it is limited, and yet it is a much sought-after metal. A painting by Rembrandt has great value because its beauty makes it desirable, and since the artist is no longer living, there will never be more of his pictures than are now in existence. Again, the supply is very limited, and the demand is great.

If we apply this rule to your relic collection or to any one item that it contains, we can come to several conclusions.

1. Indian artifacts are obviously in demand, because many private collectors, archaeologists, and anthropologists have a great interest in them.

2. As relics are found and picked up, they will become more and more scarce. The supply will continue to decrease with every passing year.
3. Whatever the worth of an artifact may be now, it is certain to increase with time. Like the Rembrandt painting mentioned above, genuine ancient Indian relics are no longer being produced!

We know that Indian artifacts are of value, and that their value will continue to increase as time goes on. But while almost all relics can be considered desirable, some of them will naturally be more valuable than others. In determining their relative worth, we can again make only very general statements. We cannot set hard and fast prices, because the monetary value of these items is always changing. But the following guidelines may help you to estimate the relative values of the artifacts in your collection.

1. Artifacts for which data is recorded are worth more than those for which it is not available.
2. A perfect specimen is always worth a great deal more than a broken or restored one of the same type.
3. The beauty of the raw material used and the quality of the workmanship on the relic will greatly influence its value. Therefore, finely crafted items such as gorgets, bannerstones, and pipes, made of materials like polished slate or rose quartz, may be worth up to 100 dollars apiece, or more. Birdstones, which are very rare and beautifully made, may sell for hundreds of dollars.
4. In general, the larger the item is, the more it will be worth. A large, fine spearhead may be valued at 60 dollars or more, whereas most small arrowheads will be worth less than 10 dollars. Small relics,

such as scrapers, knives, and drills, are rarely worth more than 5 dollars apiece.

5. The age of an artifact will partly determine its worth, although the older items are not always the most valuable ones.

For the reasons given above, you should keep your relics and try to acquire more if you can. But there are other, perhaps better, reasons than monetary gain for collecting Indian relics. And there are other ways in which value can be determined. Most people who are beginning a new hobby are not much concerned with the money and the prices involved. They start collecting because they enjoy the activities associated with their hobbies, or simply because they enjoy learning.

As a beginning collector, try to think of the worth of your artifacts in terms of the historical information that they can furnish. Your relics and the records that you keep are valuable to the study of ancient cultures, for they provide evidence from which we can form a picture of the past. By keeping a well-recorded collection, you are helping to preserve an important part of history.

When you study what has been written about the lives of prehistoric American people, you will gain a growing appreciation for the artifacts that they made. For example, a crude, partially broken projectile point made of gray rock may seem hardly worth carrying home from the field. And it might not be of any monetary value at all. But with a little study, you may discover that the item you have found once served as the point of a spear. It might be well over 4,000 years old, and it may have helped its original owner kill an elk, a bison, or a huge bear not far from the spot where you found it. Suddenly this humble bit of stone takes on new importance for you, and it may become one of the most "valuable" items in your collection.

Finally, when you determine the worth of your collection, consider the value of the friends you have made, and of the recreation and good times your hobby has given you. Unlike the uncertain worth of money, these kinds of values are unchanging and dependable.

A deeply notched flint projectile point with a restored tip

# Part two
# Cataloging
# Your Collection

The following pages provide general help in recognizing, naming, and classifying a number of Indian relics commonly found in North America. It should be emphasized that these descriptions of individual artifacts do not by any means contain detailed information. For a comprehensive treatment of the subject, the collector will want to consult more advanced sources than this one. But the descriptions and illustrations included in this section will give the beginning collector a good general picture of the kinds of artifacts that he or she is likely to find in the field.

# 9.
# Stone Tools and Ornaments

The early inhabitants of North America produced a wide variety of stone artifacts, ranging from crude fist-axes to beautifully crafted ceremonial birdstones.

The artifacts that these people made served them in all aspects of their daily lives. The early Americans manufactured countless tools, which they used for making clothing, for cultivating fields, for preparing food, and even for making other tools. They fashioned weapons for use in hunting and in war. And people of the more sophisticated cultures made fine stone artifacts for ceremonial and ornamental purposes.

The following pages describe some of the most common of these artifacts. The illustrations and brief descriptions will help the beginning collector to recognize these relics in the field and to classify them once they have become part of his or her collection.

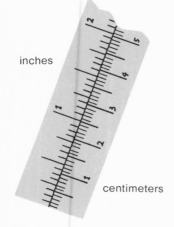

inches

centimeters

The dimensions of all artifacts are given in inches. To convert to centimeters, multiply inch measurements by 2.5.

42

## CHOPPERS

The chopper, or fist-axe, was probably one of the first tools made by humans. It remained in use in America until the arrival of the Europeans.

Choppers are difficult to recognize in the field. The percussion-flaking technique used to make them is crude, and at first a chopper may appear to be an ordinary rock. But these tools do have a roughly chipped cutting edge; directly opposite this, some very slight smoothing can be found. This smoothing was done to protect the worker's hand while the tool was in use.

The Indians used these stone choppers to hack large animals into pieces small enough to handle. Choppers were usually just large enough to be held in one hand, and they were quite heavy. In fact, their weight probably did as much to cut the meat as did the crude blade.

Choppers were made out of all kinds of stone, but slate and "greenstone" were the materials most commonly used. Choppers of flint are rarely found today.

This slate chopper measures 6-1/2 inches high and 5 inches wide.

## CELTS

A celt (SELT) is a hand-held stone axe. Unlike the chopper, the celt usually has a smooth surface and is carefully shaped, often in the form of an

43

A polished granite celt, measuring 7-1/2 inches high

elongated rectangle or triangle. Most celts were probably made by the peck-and-polish method.

For the most part, the ancient celt served the same purposes as does the present-day hatchet or hand-axe. The Indians also used the celt to split open the skulls of large animals. They did this in order to extract the brains, which were used for one step in the process of tanning hides.

This kind of work obviously required a tool made of very hard stone that would take and hold a sharp cutting edge. For this reason, celts were usually made of granite. Occasionally they were also made of flint or other stone.

## AXES

Like the celt, the stone axe is a finely crafted tool made by the peck-and-polish method. But the axe can be distinguished from the celt by the deep grooves or channels cut around its base. These grooves made it easy to lash, or haft, the axe head securely to a wooden handle. There are several varieties of stone axes, the most common of which is the "three-quarter grooved" axe. It is so named because the deep groove at the base extends only three-fourths of the way around the axe head. Axes that are "fully grooved" (grooved all the way around)

44

are less common and are probably older than other types. "Half-grooved" axes are sometimes found, but they are quite rare.

These tools are usually made of speckled granite. The pockmarked effects of the pecking method used to make them can be clearly seen on the surface of many axe heads.

*Top left*: A three-quarter grooved axe. *Top right*: The same axe, shown from the ungrooved side. This view clearly shows the wedge shape of the artifact. *Bottom*: An artist's conception of how this axe might have looked when hafted to a wooden handle.

## MAULS

The maul is a large, blunt-nosed "hammer." Mauls are almost always shaped from a granite boulder by the peck-and-polish method. Like stone axes, they may be fully grooved, three-quarter grooved, or half grooved. Unlike axes, however, mauls will usually be grooved around the middle of the stone rather than near the base.

Mauls were useful for all types of heavy pounding and crushing. They could certainly have been used as weapons, too, and they probably were at times. But their main function was almost the same as that of the modern sledge hammer.

## MULLERS AND METATES

The muller, or grinding stone, was used for crushing and pulverizing food materials. It was especially useful in grinding acorns, nutmeats, dried meat, roots, and seeds.

This simple tool comes in an endless variety of shapes, but every muller can be recognized by two distinct features: the stone will always have at least one smooth, flat side, and it will be of a size that fits easily in the hand. Often a small pit or hollow can be seen at the exact center of the flat working side. This hollow space was formed during the grinding process, when the greatest amount of wear naturally occurred at the center of the stone.

This fist-sized maul has a wide groove cut around its center.

A muller with a deeply pitted center

46

Some grinding stones were used with a metate (muh-TAH-tay or muh-TATE), a flat or dish-shaped stone bowl. The material to be ground up was piled on the metate and was then rubbed and pounded with the muller.

While mullers are very common on village and camp sites, metates are extremely rare. This would indicate that many metates were made of wood or bark and have long since rotted away.

## PESTLES

The pestle is another crushing and grinding tool. Because of its unusual shape, it is much easier to recognize than the muller. The top of a pestle is a well-formed handle, and the base, or working end, is flared. Some pestles are finely crafted, with very smooth surfaces, while others are quite crude. But they all have the same basic shape. Although several kinds of stone were used in making pestles, the majority of them were made of granite.

A bell-shaped pestle, measuring 7 inches high

Another kind of pestle is the roller pestle. As you would guess, this utensil is cylinder-shaped. It was used for pounding and also for rolling, just as modern people use a wooden rolling pin. Some roller pestles are more than 20 inches long, but most are from 8 to 12 inches in length.

## HAMMERSTONES

The primitive hammerstone is nothing more than a smooth pebble or boulder. It was held in the hand and used for pounding. Hammerstones were often used in the percussion-flaking process to shape tools and weapons.

Only the battered areas on the surface show that these stones were used by humans. Except for these rough areas, the stones are unworked and look no different from any other smooth pebbles.

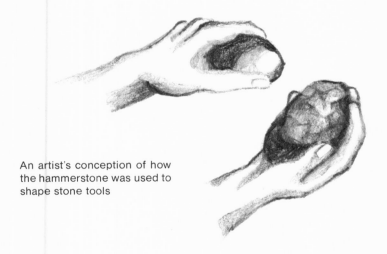

An artist's conception of how the hammerstone was used to shape stone tools

## ABRADING STONES

Abrading stones were used to smooth and polish the surfaces of various "pecked" stone artifacts and wood objects, much as sandpaper is used by modern carpenters to finish wood. Sandstone was the most commonly used abrader, because its rough but soft surface was ideal for polishing every kind of material.

Abrading stones can be found in a variety of shapes. Their surfaces are generally smooth, but sometimes deep grooves in the stones will clearly show how these artifacts were used.

## THUMB SCRAPERS

These beautiful little flint tools (sometimes referred to as *end scrapers* or *snub-nosed scrapers*) are always made in the same way. Their smooth undersides have not been worked upon by their makers. But these relics can be easily identified by the fact that one edge of the stone is always carefully chipped off by pressure-flaking to form a blunt and slightly rounded end.

Most authorities think that these tools were held between the thumb and forefinger while in use. This is why they came to be called thumb scrapers. We can be fairly sure that they were not fitted with a handle of any kind, for they never show any evidence of notching.

The use of the thumb scrapers is still uncertain. They may have been used for removing hair or flesh from animal hides, but this seems doubtful when one considers their size. Of the

Two thumb scrapers, with scraping edges shown facing left

more than 200 found by the author, the largest measures but 2-1/4 inches long by 1-3/8 inches across at the widest point. If these scrapers were ever used to clean large hides, the job would have been a slow one with such tiny tools!

Using a thumb scraper as a "spoon" for eating baked squash

Some students of Indian culture think that these stone tools were used as spoons for scraping out the edible parts of baked foods such as pumpkins and squash. Others suggest that two of them, held tightly together at the worked end, would make a fine pair of "tweezers" for the removal of unwanted facial hair!

In truth, we are unsure of just what use or uses the thumb scrapers had. The answer will come in time, but until then it is interesting to try to solve the riddle.

## SIDE SCRAPERS

The side scraper is a very common flint tool. It has been used by people in all parts of the world for thousands of years. Side scrapers have no particular shape, but every one will have at least one sharpened side. Sometimes several edges may be chipped, giving the maker a choice of cutting and scraping edges. These tools are usually large enough to fit comfortably in the palm of the hand.

A side scraper. (The scraping edge faces right.)

Side scrapers were used to clean and prepare animal skins. They were also helpful in shaping softer materials such as wood and bone. As these tools became dull, they could be resharpened by the simple method of pressure-flaking with a chipping tool of bone.

A scraper may have looked like this when hafted to a bone handle.

## HAFTED SCRAPERS

Hafted scrapers were probably used to remove hair from animal hides. These stone implements are always notched, indicating that they were usually hafted in a handle of wood or bone.

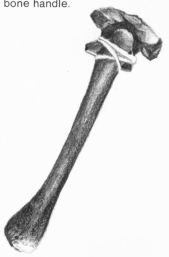

There is some question as to whether these tools were made as scrapers to begin with, or simply fashioned from broken and reworked arrowheads. To this writer, it seems logical to assume that they were made from broken arrow points. If you examine a large number of hafted scrapers, you will notice that they vary greatly in length. Some are quite long, with only a small area worked down as a scraping surface. Others are so short that the cutting edge almost meets the notches at the base. If these tools had been made to be used only as scrapers, they would be more uniform in length.

It is not difficult to imagine how an early hunter might have decided to make a scraper out of a broken arrowhead. If the hunter's arrow point broke against a rock or a tree, we can imagine how much he would have hated to throw the entire shaft away. Of course, he could have attached a new arrow point to the shaft once the broken point was cut off. But we must remember that the point was very carefully bound to the shaft with sinew. It was also glued in place with resin, pitch, or fish-skin glue. Instead of replacing the firmly attached point, the owner could simply convert it into a scraper. All that was needed to make a scraping edge was a few minutes' work with the bone flaking tool. The attached arrow shaft could then be cut off to whatever length might be desirable.

## HAND KNIVES

Hand knives and side scrapers are sometimes hard to tell apart, but there is a difference. A true stone knife will have at least one whole side sharpened,

*Top and right*: These drawings show two finely crafted stone knives mounted in wood and bone handles. *Bottom*: Cruder knives, like this 5-inch long flint blade, were held directly in the hand.

and it will often have a sharpened point as well. Knives are usually made of finer flint than are scrapers, and they will show more careful pressure-flaking. This results in a sharper, finer cutting edge.

Since flint knives were used for cutting and piercing, they were often made in nearly the same shapes as our knife blades of today. Some knives were attached to handles of wood, antler, or bone. Others were made to be held in the hand, probably with a wrapping of buckskin or rawhide to protect the worker from the flint's sharp edges.

## FLAKE KNIVES

Flake knives undoubtedly had the keenest edges of any tool made by Indians and other early people. Despite their thin, delicate appearance, these tiny knives were sturdy, and they served many useful purposes. The razor-sharp slivers could slit narrow strips from the toughest hides. They could quickly and neatly notch an arrow shaft, or trim the feathers to be used on the shaft. It is even possible that they served as primitive surgical instruments.

The flake knife was made by striking thin flakes from a specially prepared flint core. Unlike other tools struck from flint cores, these knives did not

A typical flake knife. These tools measured only 2 or 3 inches long.

Striking blades from a flint core. Once the core was prepared, several finished blades could be struck from it in a matter of minutes.

require further sharpening. The tiny flakes already had straight, sharp edges because they were split off carefully along the grain of the stone core.

The very finest and most colorful flint was used for making flake knives. Dozens of these "microlith" (tiny stone) blades could be struck from a core stone the size of a man's fist. Many collectors have cores in their collections, as well as the blades made from them.

## GRAVERS

The graver is simply a needle-sharp spur on one edge of a flint flake or chip. Sometimes thumb scrapers and side scrapers were made doubly useful by chipping a graver spur on the side opposite the prepared scraping surface.

The graver was useful for many kinds of cutting jobs. It was often used to cut thin strips of bone, which were made into needles and hair ornaments.

The graver spur is clearly visible on the lower left tip of this side scraper.

## BLANKS

Many of the early Americans depended on hunting and gathering for their livelihood. Because their way of life kept them constantly on the move, their few possessions had to be lightweight and easy to carry. For this reason, early people often worked their extra flint into blanks, which were

A flint blank, ready to be shaped into an arrow point

roughly shaped points or tools. Making these blanks helped to reduce the weight of the stone items the people carried, yet ensured them of a good supply of raw material for emergency needs.

The blank itself could be used as a scraper or a crude knife. Then, if there was need for an arrow point, a blade, or a spearhead, a few minutes' work with a chipping tool would change the blank into whatever was needed.

It should be noted that it is often difficult to absolutely identify an artifact as a blank. Many blanks bear such a close resemblance to crude knives or scrapers that it is often impossible to tell one from the other.

## DRILLS

Early people often needed to make holes in various materials. Such things as bark, soft wood, and cured hides could be pierced by any sharp implement held in the hand. But harder materials, such as stone, bone, ivory, and shell, required a better method.

Once again flint provided the answer. The early craftsman struck a long, thin drill from a core of flint. When mounted in a handle of wood, the drill could be twirled between the hands until it passed completely through the object being drilled.

As time went on, people invented

better ways of causing the drill to spin. One method, the bow-drill, worked so well that it is still used by various peoples in the world today. The early craftsman made a bow-drill from a short, springy stick that bent easily. A piece of sinew was tied from one end of the stick to the other, just as one would do in making a small bow for shooting arrows. The bowstring was then looped several times around a

An artist's conception of how the bow-drill was used. A similar apparatus, called the fire-drill, was used by many Indian people to start fires.

A flint T drill with a wide base, which the user gripped while drilling

A tiny flint thumb drill

wooden shaft, which had a stone drill point fastened to its tip. When the worker pulled the bow backward and forward, the shaft would spin rapidly, first in one direction and then in the other. A heavy stone weight held against the top of the drill shaft kept the spinning shaft steady during the drilling process. The bow-drill method allowed early craftsmen to do a neat, effective job of drilling, even in hard stone like granite.

Several varieties of stone drills were used in this and other methods of drilling. All of these drills can be easily identified by their shapes. Most of them are simply long and thin, with some kind of notching at the top (base) end. They often show much wear on the point and along the first one-third of their length. In fact, these worn surfaces can be a valuable means of identification. Many relics that are identified as drills are actually special arrowheads that look much like drill points. Only true drills will show wear, at least on the tip.

Some drills were made for use in the hand, without the aid of a handle or shaft. These are often called T drills, or thumb drills. T drills were fashioned from thin flint fragments. There was always a wide, flat area at the base that allowed the worker to hold the drill firmly between the thumb and fingers while using it.

## CUP STONES

Occasionally collectors find a stone that has small, neatly formed pits all over its surface. These stones are called cup stones, or sometimes *paint stones*, because it is believed that the Indians used them for mixing paints. There may be some truth to this theory, since these artifacts often show traces of red ochre, a type of iron ore that was used by early people for making red paint.

Experts are now quite certain that while these stone "palettes" may have been used by Indians and prehistoric Americans, they were not made by them. Instead, they were probably formed by the action of water at the bottom of a river. Skin divers have reported that such cup stones are formed when a small pebble becomes trapped in a rough spot on a slab of stone. The pebble cannot escape, and the current of the stream keeps turning and rolling it against the stone slab. After a long time the flat stone slab has a smooth cup worn into its surface.

## PLUMMETS

The plummet was so named because of its resemblance to a plumb bob, a cone-shaped weight attached to a string that carpenters use to check vertical alignment during construction.

A teardrop-shaped plummet
with a hole bored in the neck

Most stone plummets are shaped like a long teardrop and have a shallow groove around the neck or top. In some specimens, a hole is bored through the neck. Occasionally plummets are coffin-shaped, with the greatest width at the shoulder area. Whatever their shape, they range from two to four inches in length and are seldom more than one inch in diameter at their widest point. Most plummets are made of granite or hematite and have very smooth, carefully polished surfaces.

Archaeologists are unsure of the exact function of the plummet. Many think that plummets were used as bola weights for hunting. Several of these weights would have been tied to the ends of three or more strands of sinew. When whirled about the head and let fly, the stones would have carried the strings into a flock of birds, entangling their wings and bringing them down.

According to another theory, plummets were used as fishing sinkers. Some people have come to this conclusion because of the fact that these stones are often found in the dried-up beds of ancient lakes.

Objections could be raised, however, about both of these theories. Most plummets are fashioned so carefully that it must have taken a long time to finish one. After the maker had worked so hard, it seems unlikely that he or she would have risked losing such a beautiful object by throwing it far into the air, or by using it to fish in deep water. Besides, any common pebble would probably have been adequate as a bola weight or a fishing sinker.

Perhaps the plummet was intended for an entirely different purpose. Until new discoveries are made, the use of this artifact remains something of a mystery.

## HOES

Ancient stone hoes were used to till the earth for planting in much the same way that steel hoes are used today. In fact, the more carefully made hoes of chipped flint probably worked nearly as well as do our modern ones.

The finest hoes were flat, fan-shaped implements that were often notched at the top for attachment to a handle. The cruder hoes were more roughly shaped and were often unnotched.

A crude slate hoe, measuring 7-1/4 inches high

## ANVIL STONES

Anvil stones are not hard to identify. They are usually made of granite and are quite smoothly polished. The bottom side is always flat, and the top surface is hollowed out to form a shallow depression.

These stones served as working platforms for chipping stone tools and weapons or for shaping wood. They were generally useful for any projects that required a smooth, steady working surface.

## BOAT STONES

Collectors often prize their boat stones very highly. These smooth, highly polished artifacts are always beautifully made and never show any wear. They were given their name because their shapes resemble those of boats or canoes.

A boat stone made of polished slate. Most of these artifacts measured 4 to 5 inches long.

Some boat stones have holes drilled through them. This would suggest that they were either worn as ornaments or tied onto something. In any case, they probably had some ceremonial use.

While most boat stones are made of slate, some are made of granite and other types of hard stone.

## SLATE DISCS

Collectors of Indian relics have long been puzzled by the rough, flat slate discs found on known village sites. No one is quite sure what these circular stone artifacts were used for.

Slate discs are very thin, averaging perhaps three-eighths of an inch thick, and they are always of a size small enough to fit in the hand. The discs were obviously shaped by people, but they have an unfinished appearance, and their edges are jagged and uneven. There is never any evidence of grinding or polishing, even though the slate of which the discs are made polishes easily.

Many guesses have been made as to the possible uses of these discs. Some people think that they were used as "plates" for food portions. The author's opinion is that they were throwing stones. As most people know, a flat stone can be hurled through the air with great speed. Such a stone could easily have knocked down a flying duck or even a wild turkey. The throwing-stone theory would explain the rough shaping of the discs, as well as their size. They were not carefully shaped, because their makers knew that the discs would be lost when thrown far into the air. And since the discs are small, a good supply of them would have been easy to carry along on a hunting trip. However, this is

Three typical slate discs. The largest is 5 inches in diameter, and all are about 3/8 inch thick.

63

only a guess as to the use of the discs. One day the work of archaeologists may reveal their true function.

## SPUDS

The spud is a type of slate chisel that has a widely flared bit, or cutting edge. Many spuds are so well made and show such little wear that they probably were not used for common work at all. They may have been made for ceremonial or decorative purposes.

## GAME BALLS

The game ball is a most unusual artifact. Although these granite balls would be rather dangerous playthings, they are called game balls because they do resemble the balls that children play with today.

It might be more logical to assume that these carefully made relics were actually used as war-club heads. Wrapped in buckskin and lashed to long, springy handles, they would have made very good weapons. They might also have been used as bola weights, although almost any unworked stone would have served as well for this purpose.

It is amazing to discover how many different sizes of game balls were made. Some collectors specialize in collecting these unusual and varied

A typical spud. These artifacts varied in length from 6 to 13 inches.

artifacts. Most game balls show fine workmanship and are a valuable addition to any collection.

## BANNERSTONES

Bannerstones were given their name as a result of a mistake. Early collectors were unsure of the function of these well-made stone pieces, but someone eventually suggested that the relics were meant to be used as peace tokens. The theory was that the tokens were attached to the end of a stick and displayed like flags of truce when approaching an enemy.

Actually, bannerstones probably served as balance weights on spearthrower sticks. The spear-thrower, properly called an *atlatl* (aht-LAH-tl), was a short shaft made of wood, bone, or a section of antler. It had a hook at one end, which was fashioned to fit into a socket on the butt end of a spear. With an atlatl, the hunter could whip a spear forward faster and harder than was possible with the bare hands. Bannerstones attached to the atlatl would certainly have put more weight and power into the thrower's cast. The holes that are always drilled through the centers of these stones would have made it easy to attach the stones to a shaft.

Since we can safely guess that the atlatl and weights were in use before

*Top*: A "double crescent" bannerstone. *Bottom*: A "lunate" bannerstone. Both are made of banded slate.

A butterfly bannerstone made
of banded slate

the bow and arrow, we know that bannerstones are very old, and that they are of considerable archaeological importance.

Most bannerstones are made of slate. Specimens of harder stone are sometimes found, but they are very rare. Bannerstones are usually made by the peck-and-polish method, and they almost always show beautiful craftsmanship.

The most familiar of the bannerstones is the "butterfly" type. This artifact does look very much like a butterfly, but whether or not its maker was really trying to represent such an insect, we cannot tell.

A butterfly bannerstone made of banded slate

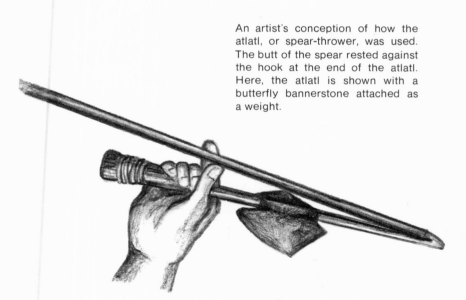

An artist's conception of how the atlatl, or spear-thrower, was used. The butt of the spear rested against the hook at the end of the atlatl. Here, the atlatl is shown with a butterfly bannerstone attached as a weight.

## BIRDSTONES

The birdstone is one of the most valuable and sought-after of all North American relics. The artistic work and the craftsmanship that these artifacts display are truly amazing!

Birdstones are most commonly made of slate. They have smooth, highly polished surfaces and show evidence of skillful use of the peck-and-polish technique. The shape is quite birdlike in most specimens. Some birdstones show only the bird's head and neck; these are called *bust* birdstones. Others have large knobs where the bird's eyes would be and are called *popeyes*. A few birdstones have a single knob worked into the top of the head. These are called *top-knots*.

There is little agreement as to the actual use of the birdstones. Some authorities think that they were worn as ornaments or that they were used with the spear-thrower (perhaps as the hook at the end of the atlatl). Others believe that they were totem symbols, identifying certain tribes or clans. There is even a persistent legend that these stone birds were thought to be able to fly a person's soul into heaven after death.

Whatever their use may have been, there is no doubt that birdstones were important to their makers. Broken specimens were reworked and redrilled so that they could be used again. Even the heads and tails were carefully saved and made useful once more. The fact that so many birdstones have been redrilled by their makers would suggest that they were used as some sort of tool rather than as an ornament.

Birdstones are rare and valuable, and most collectors hope someday to own at least one. It is often said that Indian relic collections, especially in states east of the Mississippi River, can be accurately evaluated by the number of birdstones that they contain.

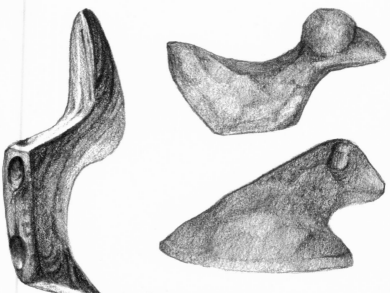

*Left*: This view shows the drilling done on the base of a typical birdstone. *Top*: A popeye birdstone. *Bottom*: A bust birdstone, sometimes called a *nesting* birdstone.

## BAR AMULETS

The bar amulet looks like a long birdstone with no head and with a tail at each end. Like the birdstone, the bar amulet is made of slate and shows evidence of great skill in working stone. In many specimens, the drilling done on each end of the amulet is identical to that done on certain types of birdstones. The purpose or use for both the birdstone and the bar amulet was probably the same, since both appear to be associated with the atlatl, or spear-thrower.

## ADZES

The stone adze, or gouge, is a chisel-like tool made of granite or flint. It was hafted in a short handle of wood or bone and positioned at a 45-degree angle to the handle. This made it very effective for rough scraping and smoothing jobs.

This tool was used primarily for shaping wood. First, sections of the wood's surface were burned. The adze was then used to gouge out the charred, softened portions. Dugout canoes were usually made in this way. It is also likely that trees were cut down by burning a part of their trunks and then chopping at the burned-out wood with an adze until the tree weakened and fell.

Bar amulets varied in length from 4 to 10 inches and were usually drilled at each end.

69

The adze is often mistakenly called a celt because of the similarity in the shape and workmanship of the two items. But the adze can be distinguished from the celt by the slight hollowing on its underside. Care should be taken to keep these two artifacts from being incorrectly labeled.

## GORGETS

The gorget (GORE-jit) is a flat, polished stone ornament made to be worn as a necklace or chestpiece. Completed gorgets are drilled, usually with two holes near the center. Some may have more than two holes, however, and others have only one.

Many gorgets are made of slate. Slate is a fragile stone, and items made from it often break. This is especially true of gorgets, which tended to break at the point of drilling. When this happened the maker would grind and polish the broken edge until it was smooth and would then redrill the ornament so that it could be used again.

A beautiful drilled gorget made of banded slate

The stone from which gorgets are made can be enhanced by rubbing it with oil or grease. Collectors find that this will bring out the soft colors within the stone. The early Americans who made these ornaments undoubtedly did the same thing, perhaps using bear grease or other animal fats.

## DISCOIDALS

The discoidal (dis-KOY-dl) is a small, doughnut-shaped stone artifact, usually made of granite or quartz. It was quite likely used as a spindle whorl, or flywheel. As such it would have helped in the job of twisting materials such as animal hair and plant fibers into coarse yarn.

Discoidals are also thought to be a type of game stone. Scholars believe they may have been used in an early version of "chunky," an Indian game popular in fairly recent times. Chunky was played by throwing spears at a rolling disc, and the discoidal may have been used as the target in this game of skill.

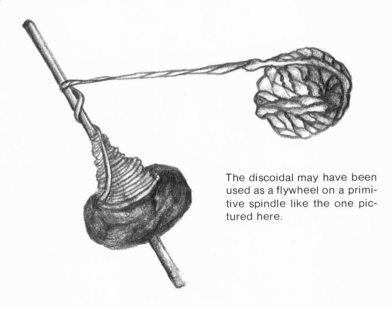

The discoidal may have been used as a flywheel on a primitive spindle like the one pictured here.

This banded slate gorget has tally marks cut all around its edges.

## TALLY MARKS

Some artifacts, especially those made of slate, have a series of small cuts around the edges. These are called tally marks. Tally marks are never very deeply cut; they were probably made by sawing across the completed artifact with a jagged-edged flint knife.

We cannot say for certain that the Indians really used these marks to keep track of things, but it is a logical guess. Some experts claim that these marks were made by grandmothers in order to record the birth of each new baby in their clans. The marks may also have recorded a person's years of age, or almost any other bits of information that the Indians needed to remember.

Of course, there is still another possibility: what we now call tally marks may have been nothing more than pure decoration.

## BEADS

The Indians and their ancestors made beads of all types. Bead necklaces and bracelets, as well as head bands with bead decoration, were worn by both men and women.

Most beads were made by sawing or cutting bird bones into button-shaped discs. Bird bones were ideal for making beads, because they were light and strong. Since they were already hollow, drilling was usually unnecessary. Other materials used for beads include stone, shell, baked clay, hammered copper, and various types of ivory from animal teeth and tusks.

## BONE ARTIFACTS

Early Americans used bone for nearly everything. It has been suggested that they really lived in the "bone age" rather than the age of stone! Because bone decays and falls apart with time, however, most of the artifacts made from it are gone forever. Even so, under certain conditions bone will last for a very long time. If it is imbedded in ashes (as is often the case with burials), or if it is in very dry ground, the bone may be preserved quite well. Many bone artifacts are found by digging in dry caves. Because we as amateurs do not do any digging, our chances of finding these artifacts are slim. But it is useful to know something about bone artifacts, because they are an important part of American archaeological history. Although many kinds of artifacts were made of bone, only a few of the most interesting items will be described in this brief summary.

Fishhooks were made by first scratching an outline of the hook on

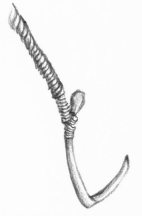

A simple bone fishhook, tied to the end of a fishing line

73

a flat, smooth section of bone, such as a rib bone. The graver spur, already described, was used for this delicate cutting job. Once the basic hook shape was cut out of the bone, it was polished and then grooved or bored so that a line could be attached. Most fishhooks were not barbed.

Arrow and harpoon points of bone are not common, but they may be seen in museums and in some private collections. They were fashioned by splitting a large bone and then shaping the sharp splinters with tools of flint.

Flakers for working flint were made from a smooth, hard section of solid bone. These are small—usually about the length and shape of a person's finger. Bone flakers were held in the hand. They were used in the pressure-flaking process to chip tiny flakes of flint from the surfaces and edges of arrowheads, knives, scrapers, and other flint weapons and tools.

Hairpins and other ornaments of bone are often found during excavations of camp and burial sites. Some hairpins may be more than 10 inches in length. They are always highly polished and quite artistically made.

Early Americans also made needles out of bone. Some bone needles are so similar to the large, smooth needles in use today that they need no description. Others, often made from the leg

A bone flaking tool, hafted to a wooden handle

bones of birds, are heavy and thick, with a large hole, or "eye." These needles may have been used for sewing tough skins and bark.

## EFFIGY POINTS

As early people became more skillful in working with flint, some cultures began to make very elaborate flint arrowheads and other articles. These strange-looking effigy (EFF-ih-jee) points, sometimes called *eccentric points*, were finely crafted and were probably used for special ceremonies. They were made to be decorative rather than functional.

Whatever their exact purpose, these special projectile points give evidence of the early Americans' remarkable skill in shaping fine flint.

A fine example of a black flint effigy point

## PIPES

Early inhabitants of North and South America were among the first people in the world to use tobacco. Pipes for smoking tobacco (and probably other leaves and grasses as well) can often be found on ancient camp and village sites.

Pipes, both simple and elaborate, were used by various tribes and cultures. The simplest was called a *tube pipe*. It was merely a hollowed stone or clay tube that was stuffed with tobacco. It must have looked much like a cigar when being smoked. Most pipes were made in an elbow shape, quite similar to pipes being made today.

The most beautiful pipes have been found with the burials of chiefs and important people. These are made of pipestone, slate, soapstone, or other types of stone. Such pipes are often carved in the images of animals, birds, or humans. Most of these *effigy pipes* are quite small. The average length is about three and one-half inches.

Sacred ceremonial pipes, sometimes called *peace pipes*, were much larger. These were priceless tribal possessions and were highly decorated.

*Top:* An effigy pipe, probably representing the figure of a bird. *Center:* A simple tube pipe. *Bottom:* An elbow pipe, similar to a modern pipe.

## COPPER TOOLS

Metal tools made by early people are much less common than tools made of stone and bone. But crude copper artifacts are sometimes found in certain areas of the country. The items most commonly found are knives, needles, projectile points, axes, gouges, and chisels.

The Indians usually found the copper for making these tools and weapons on the surface of the ground. There are some early copper mining areas, however, where the crude pits are still visible. Most of these mines are located near Lake Superior.

Most copper artifacts were simply beaten into shape with hammerstones. In some cases, there is evidence that the copper was heated and cooled in order to harden the metal. This process, called *annealing*, is still used today.

Two potshards, showing the rough outside surface of the vessel (top), and the smooth inner surface (bottom).

## POTTERY

Whenever archaeologists find pottery at a given location, they can be pretty certain that the people who lived there had a settled way of life. The hunting and wandering people of very early times did not use much pottery, because it was easily broken while traveling. But people who settled down to an agricultural way of life could afford to make and use pottery vessels.

The Indians took the clay for their pottery from river or lake bottoms. The clay was *tempered* (made stronger) by adding fine gravel or crushed shells while it was still wet.

Indian pottery was made by hand, usually by the coil method. The worker made long coils of clay and circled one on top of the other until the pot was built up to the desired height. The pot was then baked by putting it in the middle of a hot fire. Sometimes the finished pot would be decorated by painting it, usually with white, black, or red paint. It might also be decorated by scratching a design into its surface before baking.

Relic hunters rarely find complete pottery objects today. They usually find pieces of broken pottery, called *shards* or *sherds*. These potshards are easy to recognize in the field. If a shard is lying with its inside surface up, it will appear smooth and concave. If the outside surface is visible, a rough pattern of indentations will show clearly on the convex curvature of the piece.

Often after heavy rains, exposed potshards will dissolve slightly, causing a discoloration of the surrounding soil. This coloring (usually yellow or reddish) is a helpful clue to watch for when searching for pottery.

# 10.
# Projectile Points

The name *arrowheads* is often given to a great number of artifacts that may or may not have been fastened to the tip of an arrow shaft. Many of the smaller points, for example, were dart tips, used with a detachable shaft and spear-thrower. Others served as spear-heads or knives. Because these arti-facts were not always made to be used as arrow points, archaeologists prefer to call them *projectile points*.

In this section, you will find descrip-tions of 19 different kinds of projectile points. While most of these points were made in the same general way, different cultures had their own unique methods of finishing each point. You must study the details of each point in your collection very carefully in order to distinguish one kind of point from another.

First, feel the artifact to test for ground or polished areas. A smooth polish will most often be found on the base or the tang of the point. The base itself may be either concave, convex, or square in shape.

Next, hold the point at eye level, with one end toward you, to determine its shape in cross section. Is it thin or thick? Does it have a ridge, or spine, down the center? Are either of the edges beveled (sloping)?

The notching (or absence of notching, in some cases) should be noted

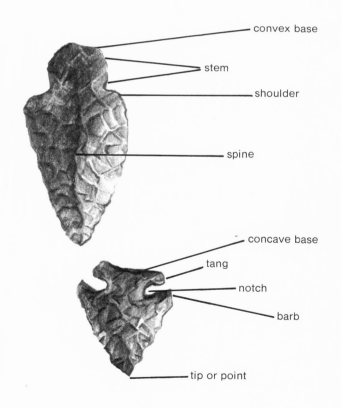

convex base

stem

shoulder

spine

concave base

tang

notch

barb

tip or point

next. Sometimes the notches have been cut in such a way that a barb is formed on each shoulder of the point. In other cases, the notching forms a rounded shoulder only. Notches may be cut in the sides of the point, in the corners, or in the base. Some notches are deep and curving, whereas others are shallow and broad. Look carefully at the notches on your artifacts and learn to recognize each kind.

You may assume that, unless otherwise described, the weapon tips discussed in this section are normally made of flint or closely related types of stone. Since most of the points are made of similar materials, the shape and workmanship will usually be the deciding factors in classifying your points.

The discussion in the following pages does not include a complete listing of the many varieties of weapon tips found in North America. Those mentioned are, however, some of the best-known and most commonly recognized types.

## ADENA

The Adena spear point is fairly broad and flat. It has no notches or barbs, and its base is long and rounded. Because of the shape of its base, this point is sometimes called the *beavertail.*

Note the careful chipping done on this Adena spear point.

## HOPEWELL

The people of the ancient Hopewell culture produced some of the most beautiful of all the projectile points. These points are always made of colorful varieties of flint, and they display workmanship of the finest quality.

One type of Hopewell point—the *dovetail*—is shaped somewhat like a teardrop. This point shows evidence of grinding on the base, which may be either concave or convex. The inner surfaces of the neat, narrow notches are often polished as well.

## SIDE-NOTCHED

Several cultures manufactured the side-notched point. It is known to be a very old type, and one that people continued to make for a long period of time. Most true side-notched points show some grinding on the base. They are square-stemmed, and their notches are often quite deep and broad.

## BIFURCATED

The bifurcated projectile point is another very old point type. The base is extended and is so deeply notched that it appears to be cut in two parts (*bifurcated* means "cut in half"). These points are often very short and flat, with pointed shoulders. There are many variations of the bifurcated point, but all of them are easy to recognize because of their unusual bases. Another name for the bifurcated point is the *Lecroy point*.

## TRIANGULAR

Collectors often refer to triangular points as *war points*. According to a persistent legend, these points were used only for warfare—never for hunting.

Triangular points are unnotched, and it is said that they were simply fitted into a split arrow shaft without any binding. When the arrow struck flesh and the shaft was pulled out, the stone point remained imbedded in the unlucky warrior who had been hit.

It is known that the triangular arrow point was made by the Erie tribe. It has not yet been proven, however, that the Erie used these points only for war.

## TURKEY TAIL

The turkey tail point was probably a spear or knife point. This artifact gets its name from its unique notching, which forms a small base shaped somewhat like the tail of a turkey.

These blades are often found in caches (underground hiding places) or with burials.

## BIRD POINTS

Some projectile points are very tiny —less than one-half inch long. Collectors call them bird points because it is thought that they were used for shooting at birds and other small game. The theory is that such tiny points would have killed small animals without destroying much of their meat.

Many of these weapon tips are beautifully made, often of the finest material.

This photograph shows 12 tiny bird points of various types. Despite their small size, these points are finely worked in every detail.

## ARCHAIC BEVEL

As its name implies, the archaic bevel point dates back to very ancient times. This point has pronounced shoulders and a fan-shaped base. The edge of the base is usually polished, as are the bases of most very old points.

An archaic bevel point was made by chipping one edge until it was sharp, and then chipping the other edge from the opposite face of the point. This method produces a raised spine on each face of the point and gives the point its peculiar, twisted appearance.

## BLUNTS

True blunts are quite rare. They were used for stunning small game, and for this reason they are also called *stunners*. These points were undoubtedly salvaged from broken arrow points that were reworked into a blunt, rounded edge.

## SERRATED POINTS

*Serrations* are deep, regular notches along the edges of a projectile point. Most points have a small degree of serration, but on some types the notches are very deep. The notched edges of such arrow tips would have torn a ragged hole in whatever they struck.

## FLUTED POINTS

These projectile points can always be recognized by the groove, or flute, that is chipped along the middle of the point, from the base toward the tip. This flute was cut to allow attachment of a shaft or handle.

There are several kinds of fluted points. One of the earliest and most widely made is the Clovis point. Others are the Folsom, Scottsbluff, Quad, Cumberland, Eden, and Dalton

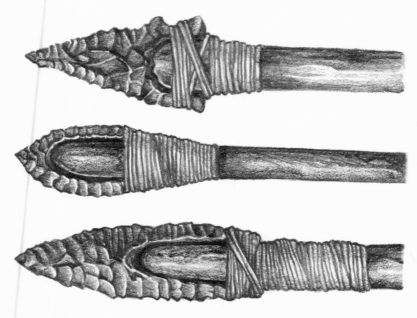

Three fluted points, shown hafted on wooden spear shafts. *Top*: A Dalton point with a small, rounded flute. *Center*: A Folsom point. Its flute extends almost the entire length of the point. *Bottom*: A Clovis point with a long, narrow flute.

varieties. The Folsom is the most striking of all these points, because the flute extends the full length of the point.

It is certain that these points were used as spearheads and dart tips. They were probably made long before the invention of the bow and arrow. We know that they are very ancient, because they have been found with the bones of animals that have been extinct for thousands of years. In fact, the Clovis points from New Mexico, which were made about 12,000 years ago, are some of the oldest artifacts found in North America. These points have helped archaeologists to estimate when humans first came to this continent.

Because of their great age and archaeological importance, fluted projectile points are much sought-after by collectors. It is a lucky field hunter who finds one! Care should be taken, however, in identifying fluted artifacts. Many points that appear to be fluted have merely been thinned at the base by their makers.

## LEVANNA

This small, triangular projectile point resembles the Erie point. The Levanna, however, has a much wider base, and its base is deeply concave rather than squared-off.

The Levanna point has a deeply concave base.

### CAHOKIA

These arrowheads from the Midwest are unmistakable. They are shaped like triangular war points, but they have deep notches on both edges at the shoulder area, and often an additional notch in the center of the base.

### STEMMED POINTS

The stemmed arrow point has no notches. The base is simply a squared-off projection, and the shoulders are very small and rounded.

### AFTON

The Afton point is often referred to as the *pentagonal point*, because it appears to be five-sided. This is due to the distinct extra shoulder on the edge of the point.

This Afton point has an extra shoulder on its left edge.

## FRACTURE BASE

This arrowhead is found only in the Ohio Valley. It is shaped roughly like an isosceles triangle. The fracture-base point was given its name because the base was deliberately snapped off by the maker when the point was completed.

## YUMA

The Yuma is a very ancient point that was used as a spearhead. Some Yuma points have square, blunt bases that have been carefully ground. Others have no bases at all.

These long, straight-edged points are often chipped in a diagonal pattern called *collateral flaking*. This chipping and flaking is often very beautiful and shows evidence of great skill in working stone.

## COLUMBIA GEM POINTS

These arrowheads are certainly the most valuable stone relics found in North America, because they are made of semi-precious stones like the fire opal. Gem points were made in a variety of shapes. The most distinctive shape is that of the Columbia River gem point. Other gem points have a triangular shape and resemble the Erie and Cahokia weapon tips.

## ASHTABULA

These artifacts can be easily recognized by their deep, graceful notches. The Ashtabula point has no barbs, and its shoulders are gently rounded. The base is much narrower than the widest part of the point.

Three Ashtabula points. The specimen below is fashioned from an unusual piece of two-colored flint.

# An Invitation to
# Further Study

Because this book is meant as a beginner's guide to the hobby of collecting Indian relics, it does not deal with all the specific details of classification. In fact, only brief mention has been made of the many types and classes of stone artifacts. But more detailed books and pamphlets have been written on this and related subjects, and consulting these sources will be the next step for a collector who wants to learn more about the artifacts in his or her collection.

This book has also dealt only briefly with items other than those made of stone—the bone artifacts, copper tools, beads, and pottery made by people of ancient cultures. And no mention has been made of *trade goods*, the relics that were originally manufactured and brought to North America by Europeans. The research and study possibilities in this field are endless, because the Indians possessed a great many of these trade items. Articles such as glass beads, metal axes, metal hoes, jewelry, guns, knives, kettles, and utensils were in common use and can still be found today.

No matter what kinds of artifacts interest you most, you will find that learning about their history can be almost as exciting as finding the artifacts themselves. Study and research will not only help you to become more knowledgeable about the Indians and their ancestors, but will also make you a more successful field hunter. As you learn more about the habits and customs of the early Americans, you will become more and more successful at discovering the artifacts that they made. You will find that you will waste much less time searching areas that are unlikely to produce any relics and that you will have an easier time spotting relics in the field.

Now that you have read this brief guide, and perhaps other books as well, you are ready to start your new hobby. Like any hobby, collecting Indian relics requires patience and time. But if you are willing to put in a little extra effort, you will be rewarded with a pastime that will intrigue and entertain you now, and for many years to come.

# Supplementary Readings

Brennan, Louis A. *American Dawn: A New Model of American Prehistory*. New York: The Macmillan Company, 1970. The author uses recent archaeological evidence to support his new and sometimes startling theories about American prehistory. Includes a useful bibliography.

Ceram, C.W. *The First American: A Story of North American Archaeology*. New York: Harcourt Brace Jovanovich, Inc., 1971. Describes the work of many major archaeologists and presents the story of the American past as it has been revealed through their findings. Illustrated, with an extensive bibliography.

Claiborne, Robert. *The First Americans*. The Emergence of Man. New York: Time Inc., 1973. Traces the origins and development of North America's prehistoric inhabitants, from the earliest wandering tribes to the sophisticated Mound Builder cultures. Beautifully illustrated.

Driver, Harold E. *Indians of North America*. Chicago: University of Chicago Press, 1961. A study of the living patterns of a wide variety of Indian tribes and culture groups that existed in North America from the 16th to the 19th centuries. Illustrated.

Josephy, Alvin M., Jr. *The Indian Heritage of America*. New York: Alfred A. Knopf, 1971. An outstanding reference book that traces the history and culture of native North, Central, and South American peoples from prehistory through the present day. Illustrated, with an excellent bibliography.

Kroeber, Theodora. *Ishi in Two Worlds: A Biography of the Last Wild Indian in North America.* Los Angeles: University of California Press, 1961. The fascinating story of Ishi, the last surviving member of the Yahi Indian Tribe, who left his Stone Age world and learned to adapt to 20th-century life. Illustrated.

Miles, Charles. *Indian and Eskimo Artifacts of North America.* Chicago: Henry Regnery Company, 1963. A fine reference work that makes many interesting comparisons between present-day Eskimo implements and similar artifacts from prehistoric North America. Illustrated.

Schneider, Richard C. *Crafts of the North American Indians.* New York: Van Nostrand Reinhold Company, 1972. This unusual book teaches readers how to make a variety of American Indian artifacts, including hand-chipped stone tools. All instructions are clearly illustrated and easy to follow.

Tunis, Edwin. *Indians.* Cleveland: The World Publishing Company, 1959. Although the text of this book offers only general information about the American Indians, the author's detailed line drawings are highly informative.

## Acknowledgments

All artifacts shown in photographs are from the author's personal collection, with the exception of the following items: Mark Buehrer collection, pp. 34, 44; Peter Diller collection, pp. 60, 62, 65 (top and bottom), 66 (top), 70, 72, 75, 81, 82 (top), 90 (top left); Gilbert Walls collection, pp. 27 (right), 45 (top left and right), 46 (top).

# Index